DEAR YOUNG ME

Written by Joy Harris-Bird

Copyright © 2021

All Rights Reserved

No part of this book may be reproduced in any form or by any electronic or mechanical means, including information storage and retrieval systems, without written permission from the author, except for the use of brief quotations in a book review.

Bright Light Publishing, LLC

ISBN 978-0-578-89015-9

Acknowledge Your Pain

ac·knowl·edge
/əkˈnälej/

verb
1. accept or admit the existence or truth of.

I was on a path of self-destruction. I blamed anyone and everyone for my pain. It's almost as if I wanted them to feel as broken as I did. I would bottle up all of my emotions to shield myself from being hurt. Sound familiar?

I was viewed as mean, but inside I felt that my life didn't have meaning. I refused to acknowledge the very thing that caused me to feel this way. I would cover it up with clothes and superficial things, but that wasn't working for me anymore.

There are not enough material things to cover up the wounds of a broken past.

I had to determine the root cause of my hurt. Trust me; I know that's easier said than done. It is difficult to address issues that you have spent years suppressing. However, you have to take the band-aid off at some point so the wound can begin to heal. It was in a challenging moment of self-reflection that I realized that everyone else was not the problem. It was me. That's not to say that I hadn't been hurt by others. I did, however, give them more power by holding on to the pain.

Once I acknowledged it, the healing journey began.

The beauty of the journey is not found in the destination, but in the steps, you take along the way!

Reflection

What past hurt are you holding to? What steps can you take to move forward?

_____
_____
_____
_____
_____
_____
_____
_____
_____
_____
_____
_____
_____
_____
_____

Heal me, LORD, and I will be healed; save me and I will be saved, for you are the one I praise.

Jeremiah 17:14

QUOTE OF THE DAY

"If you never mute the noise from the crowd, you won't be able to hear the sound of your calling."

TODAY I AM GRATEFUL FOR:

HEALING AFFIRMATION

I GIVE MYSELF PERMISSION TO HEAL

WRITE YOUR OWN AFFIRMATION

NOTES

> ACKNOWLEDGING PAIN IS THE FIRST STEP IN MOVING BEYOND IT.

Weekly Goals

Congratulations! You have taken the first step in healing. The process of acknowledging your inner child involves recognizing and accepting things that caused you pain in childhood. Your goal this week is to write one thing every day you have learned about yourself so far. Don't forget to also write a few positive affirmations!

MONDAY

TUESDAY

WEDNESDAY

THURSDAY

FRIDAY

SATURDAY

SUNDAY

don't forget...

Feel All The Feelings

I would love to tell you that I acknowledged my pain, and I was instantly healed. However, it didn't quite happen that way. When I finally opened that jar of emotions, everything fell out. I was forced to dig deeper into the broken pieces of me. Healing your inner child means releasing all of the causes of your childhood pain to adequately live life as an adult.

I can recall having a conversation with my husband. We had been married for about 6 months at this time. We were not arguing, but there was something different in his tone of voice. At the time, I didn't know about triggers, but I was about to find out. Before I knew it, I was in tears, and I didn't know why. I was flooded with all of these different feelings, and I didn't know how to process them. I became upset with myself for getting emotional over something so small. I felt as if I had faced a significant setback in my journey.

I took a moment and allowed myself to feel all of those feelings.

I realized that feelings are essential on your journey of healing. My reaction to my husband caused me to dig deeper into the cause of those emotions.

Why? When? How? I had to look deep inside and answer these difficult questions. Digging deep means getting uncomfortable to change and grow.

The healing journey is challenging. The good news is that you are not alone! God is there with you every step of the way. You just have to do the work!

I promise the reward will be worth it in the end.

Reflection

How can you dig deeper into your past to heal your inner child?

_____
_____
_____
_____
_____
_____
_____
_____
_____
_____
_____
_____
_____
_____
_____
_____
_____

Be strong and courageous, and do the work. Do not be afraid or discouraged, for the L<small>ORD</small> God, my God, is with you.

1 Chronicles 28:20

QUOTE OF THE DAY

"Sometimes a change of perspective is all it takes to see the light."

TODAY I AM GRATEFUL FOR:

HEALING AFFIRMATION

I'M WILLING TO SEE THINGS DIFFERENTLY

WRITE YOUR OWN AFFIRMATION

NOTES

> **THE BEST AND MOST BEAUTIFUL THINGS IN THE WORLD CANNOT BE SEEN OR EVEN TOUCHED. THEY MUST BE FELT WITH THE HEART.**

Weekly Goals

This week I want you to focus on your feelings! Sometimes, we don't want to deal with those tough emotions. However, it is necessary in order to be fully healed and whole. Write down how you are feeling each day this week. Don't forget to write down something positive that happened!

MONDAY

TUESDAY

WEDNESDAY

THURSDAY

FRIDAY

SATURDAY

SUNDAY

don't forget...

Let Go Of The Past

One of the worst things that we can do is hold on to the past. This could be your past mindset or past circle of friends. You have to let it go. There will always be someone who remembers who you used to be.

For the longest time, I struggled with letting go. I was surrounded by people who knew who I once was, and it was preventing me from being who I had become. It is hard to truly move forward when you are weighed down with the burden of the past.

There was a point in my journey that seemed as if I was frozen in time. I wasn't who I used to be, but there was more to who I could become. I had dreams and ideas, but I felt like no one believed in the "new me." I began to question who I was. I realized that I had carried my old mindset into my new life. It's like I was trying to soar with one foot chained to the ground. I let the opinions of others stop me from pursuing my purpose.

I had to mute the noise from the crowd, so I could hear the sound of my calling.

Letting go of my past gave me freedom. I was free to pursue my passion and soar towards my future.

You have to leave who you were. Love who you are and look forward to who you will become!

Your future is waiting!

Reflection

What are some areas in your life that you need to let go of? How is your mindset hindering your growth?

_____
_____
_____
_____
_____
_____
_____
_____
_____
_____
_____
_____

Therefore, if anyone is in Christ, the new creation has come: The old has gone, the new is here!

2 Corinthians 5:17

QUOTE OF THE DAY

"If you want to fly, you have to let go of things that weigh you down."

TODAY I AM GRATEFUL FOR:

HEALING AFFIRMATION

I AM READY TO FORGIVE ANYONE THAT I FEEL HAS HURT ME

WRITE YOUR OWN AFFIRMATION

NOTES

> I REALIZE THERE'S SOMETHING INCREDIBLY HONEST ABOUT TREES IN WINTER, HOW THEY'RE EXPERTS AT LETTING THINGS GO!

Weekly Goals

Letting go of the past isn't easy. This week I want you to write down one thing every day that you are going to let go of! Don't forget to write a milestone you have experienced so far!

MONDAY

TUESDAY

WEDNESDAY

THURSDAY

FRIDAY

SATURDAY

SUNDAY

don't forget...

Be Easy On Yourself

proc·ess
/ˈprä ses,ˈprō ses/

noun,
1. a series of actions or steps taken in order to achieve a particular end

If you know me there is one word that I will NEVER use. I cringe when anyone says it and I overall do not like it. That word is fat. There is something about it that triggers all of my emotions. I was teased and bullied in school because of my weight and that was their word of choice. I would hide out in the bathroom stall just to have a moment of peace from the constant bullying.

I thought it wouldn't bother me with my new mindset but I was wrong. One day, I was in the grocery store, shopping and minding my own business when a little boy said it. It's something about hearing that word that takes me back to my childhood. I instantly became that little girl crying in the bathroom stall. I was down for a few days and began practicing old behaviors of isolation.

I turned to God in prayer and he began mending my broken heart. I realized I had given one-word complete power over my life. I was so disappointed that I had allowed this setback to happen.

However, you cannot have a setback unless you have already made progress.

It was in this moment of brokenness that God reminded me of who I am. He told me I am loved more than I would ever know. I had to learn to take it easy on myself. Setbacks will happen but it is all part of the process. The process is not just one step; it is multiple steps taken to reach your goal.

You have to commit to healing and trust that you will be better in the end!

Reflection

Are there moments that you are too hard on yourself? How can you improve?

_____
_____
_____
_____
_____
_____
_____
_____
_____
_____
_____
_____
_____
_____

And walk in love as Christ loved us and gave himself up for us.

Ephesians 5:2

QUOTE OF THE DAY

"You are allowed to be both a masterpiece and a work in progress simultaneously."

TODAY I AM GRATEFUL FOR:

HEALING AFFIRMATION

I AM CAPABLE OF UNCONDITIONAL LOVE

WRITE YOUR OWN AFFIRMATION

NOTES

> **SHE REMEMBERED WHO SHE WAS AND THE GAME CHANGED!**

Weekly Goals

You are doing amazing! Remember, slow progress is STILL progress! This week write about something positive that happened every day. Don't forget to write about one thing you did for YOU this week!

MONDAY

TUESDAY

WEDNESDAY

THURSDAY

FRIDAY

SATURDAY

SUNDAY

don't forget...

Learn To Forgive

I can remember being contacted by one of the girls who bullied me in school. She wasn't reaching out to apologize but to ask for my help. She was thinking about changing careers and wanted me to write her resume. I just sat there for a moment as all of the memories from school came flooding back. I was angry that she even decided to message me anything. I decided that I wouldn't respond and went on about my day.

A couple of days went by and this message was haunting me. If I was truly healed, why was I unable to address her? The problem was I had never forgiven her. I was still holding on to something that happened years ago.

Truth is, the forgiveness wasn't for her; it was for me.

Anyone can hold a grudge, but it takes true character to forgive. Forgiveness doesn't mean you forget about what happened. It simply means that you have made peace with the pain and you're ready to let it go.

You also need to learn to forgive yourself. I could have handled this situation better. However, I am not perfect. I will make mistakes and that's okay.

You have to allow yourself space to fall and grace once you get back up!

Reflection

Is there someone that you are struggling to forgive? What steps can you take to move forward?

_____
_____
_____
_____
_____
_____
_____
_____
_____
_____
_____
_____

It's wise to be patient and show what you are like by forgiving others.

Proverbs 19:11

QUOTE OF THE DAY

To forgive is to set a prisoner free and discover that the prisoner was you."

TODAY I AM GRATEFUL FOR:

HEALING AFFIRMATION

I SET MYSELF AND OTHERS FREE BY LEARNING TO FORGIVE

WRITE YOUR OWN AFFIRMATION

NOTES

> **FORGIVENESS DOES NOT CHANGE THE PAST, BUT IT DOES ENLARGE THE FUTURE!**

HEAL YOUR INNER CHILD ACTIVITY

For this activity, you will write a letter addressing all of the things you would say to your inner child. During this journey of healing, you will notice that you begin to accept yourself better and feel more complete.

Dear Young Me,

Mindset Shift

Your imperfections make you beautiful. It's time to change your perspective. Rewrite your negative beliefs into a new empowering perspective.

Limited Belief	Empowering Belief
Example: I am not good enough	I am a too big of a gift to this world to waste time worrying about my imperfections.

Find Love Again

One of the hardest things that you can do after being hurt is to love again. Once your heart has been broken, you want to do whatever you can to protect it. When I first started dating my husband, I was very reluctant to let him in. I created a huge wall that not even the strongest warrior could get through. I kept my conversation vague and I bottled up all of my emotions.

However, suppressing my emotions led to physical pain.

One day, my husband and I were watching a movie and I felt like my chest was going to cave in. I became short of breath and lightheaded. He asked me what was wrong and I laid my head on his shoulder and just started talking. I began to tell him about everything that I had been going through. When I finished talking, I felt a huge weight lifted off of my shoulders. However, I was scared of how he would react. I had just emotionally dumped several years of pain on him in a matter of minutes. He just hugged me and told me that everything would be okay.

I was afraid of opening my heart but it turned out to be the best decision I could make. It takes great strength to look past what you've been through and trust someone new not to put you through it again. When you peel back the layers of your brokenness, you will find a beautiful heart that is ready and willing to love again.

Heal, and give your inner child a chance to experience love.

The greatest act of courage is not learning to love but despite everything choosing to love again!

Reflection

Are you still suppressing your emotions? How can you move forward in order to receive love?

_____
_____
_____
_____
_____
_____
_____
_____
_____
_____
_____
_____
_____

"Whoever does not love does not know God, because God is love."

1 John 4:8

QUOTE OF THE DAY

"The happiness of your life depends upon the quality of your thoughts."

TODAY I AM GRATEFUL FOR:

HEALING AFFIRMATION

I AM WILLING TO GIVE THE LOVE I EXPECT FROM OTHERS

WRITE YOUR OWN AFFIRMATION

NOTES

> **FALL IN LOVE WITH HEALING YOURSELF!**

Weekly Goals

Last weeks' activity was all about changing your mindset. Your goal this week is to put your new empowered mind to work. Write down one empowering affirmation each day. Recite it to yourself as you go about your day! Don't forget to write about how are you feeling this week!

MONDAY

TUESDAY

WEDNESDAY

THURSDAY

FRIDAY

SATURDAY

SUNDAY

don't forget...

Pull The Trigger

trig·ger
/ˈtriɡər/

verb
1. cause (an event or situation) to happen or exist.

I didn't know anything about triggers until I got into a serious relationship. Emotional triggers are the surprises that we get when someone we love, or a situation, causes us to have a reaction that we haven't processed yet

Growing up, my father struggled with alcohol addiction. There were times that he would raise his voice at me in anger. You don't realize how these things affect you until you get older. I spoke earlier about my husband elevating his tone with me. He wasn't yelling but it took me back to a moment in my childhood. I felt like the little girl being reprimanded by her father and I didn't like it. My husband was pulling on a trigger that I didn't know existed.

Your emotional triggers are old wounds that need to heal. Trust me; I know that is easier said than done. The first thing you have to do is realize what is happening now is not what happened then. Next, you have to determine what you were feeling at that moment and rid yourself of that belief. For me, I felt helpless as a child but that was no longer the case. I replaced that negative feeling with a positive one. I went from feeling helpless to feeling powerful.

You have the power to control your emotions and how you respond when triggered.

Once you release your old triggers you can view the world from an entirely different place instead of through the eyes of your scared inner child.

"Time does heal all wounds but not until after the wounds have been felt."

Reflection

Are you aware of your emotional triggers? What steps can you take to begin healing your old wounds?

_____
_____
_____
_____
_____
_____
_____
_____
_____
_____
_____
_____

"LORD my God, I called to you for help, and you healed me."

Psalm 30:2

| QUOTE OF THE DAY |

"Even the smallest shift in perspective can bring about the greatest healing."

TODO I AM GRATEFUL FOR:

HEALING AFFIRMATION

I ACCEPT THE LESSON MY PAIN IS OFFERING ME.

WRITE YOUR OWN AFFIRMATION

NOTES

> **BE GRATEFUL FOR TRIGGERS, THEY POINT WHERE YOU ARE NOT FREE!**

Weekly Goals

You are making progress! This week I want you to focus on your emotions. Each day write down how you are feeling. Was there a specific action that caused you to feel this way? Use this week to dig deeper into your emotions and identify your triggers. Don't forget to write about something positive that happened this week!

MONDAY

TUESDAY

WEDNESDAY

THURSDAY

FRIDAY

SATURDAY

SUNDAY

don't forget...

Create A Space For Healing

space
/spās/

the distance from other people or things that a person needs in order to remain comfortable

Healing requires space. Most of us see this as physical but it is also internal. Our inner space can become crowded with thoughts, beliefs, and judgments that keep us from healing.

For years, I believed that I couldn't become anything more than what I already was. My inner space was filled with negative words that were spoken to me over throughout my life. These thoughts made it impossible for me to heal. I had to silence the noise and remove the clutter so I could finally begin to move forward.

I did this by creating a physical space in my home. I turned my closet into my sacred space. I went to the store and purchased a candle, notebook, desk lamp, and bean bag pillow. Next, I brought in an old end table to put my items on. I also had an old dry erase board that I hung on the wall. I used it to write affirmations, scriptures, prayer requests, and my daily goals.

Once my physical space was ready, it was time to work on myself internally. I began to remove my limiting beliefs and replaced them with empowering ones. I turned to the word of God to determine who I was and applied that to my life. I made room for God to enter my heart and mend those areas that were broken.

Truth is, you have the internal space to heal. You just have to be willing to let go of some of the clutter and silence the noise of your mind!

When you create space, you create possibility. It is an invitation to joy, fulfillment, and true healing.

Reflection

Is your inner space crowded with negative thoughts and beliefs? What steps can you take to remove those thoughts?

_____
_____
_____
_____
_____
_____
_____
_____
_____
_____
_____

Very early in the morning, while it was still dark, Jesus got up, left the house and went off to a solitary place, where he prayed."

Mark 1:35

QUOTE OF THE DAY

"When you let go, you're creating space for something better."

TODAY I AM GRATEFUL FOR:

HEALING AFFIRMATION

I AM WILLING TO AMEND MY OWN BEHAVIOR

WRITE YOUR OWN AFFIRMATION

NOTES

> "THE SOUL NEEDS MORE SPACE THAN THE BODY."

Weekly Goals

This week is all about self-care. Write down one thing you have done for yourself each day! Don't forget to write about how you are feeling at this point in your journey.

MONDAY

TUESDAY

WEDNESDAY

THURSDAY

FRIDAY

SATURDAY

SUNDAY

don't forget...

Healing Doesn't Happen Overnight

heal·ing
/ˈhēliNG/

1. the process of making or becoming sound or healthy again.

Healing is a process, not a race. The deeper the wound, the longer it will take to heal.

When someone loses a limb, they often experience something called phantom pain. They feel the pain as if the limb is still there. One of the options to treat phantom pain is mirror therapy. This treatment method uses vision to give the brain the illusion that the limb is still there and moving. You can use this same method while on your journey of healing. You have to see it first!

Believing in something before you see it is contrary to human nature. We've been conditioned to see things first, and then believe. However, faith is to believe in what you do not see. The reward of this faith is to see what you believe.

On my journey, I have visualized myself healed and whole. However, there were some days that I did not feel that way. One wrong word or action from a friend or loved one could trigger a sea of emotions. I had to realize that healing does not happen overnight. Every day you have to take one step towards being who you were always meant to be.

You will always have a scar from your wound, how you treat is up to you.

Reflection

How has your faith impacted your healing? What steps can you take to strengthen your faith?

_____
_____
_____
_____
_____
_____
_____
_____
_____
_____
_____
_____

Now faith is being sure of what we hope for and certain of what we do not see.

Hebrews 11:1

QUOTE OF THE DAY

"Healing doesn't mean the damage never existed. It means the damage no longer controls our lives."

TODAY I AM GRATEFUL FOR:

HEALING AFFIRMATION

I TRUST THAT EVERYTHING IN MY LIFE IS UNFOLDING PERFECTLY

WRITE YOUR OWN AFFIRMATION

NOTES

> **HEALING IS AN ART.**
>
> **IT TAKES TIME.**
>
> **IT TAKES PATIENCE.**
>
> **IT TAKES LOVE.**

Weekly Goals

You are doing awesome! I know some days are harder than others, but you have to keep going. This week I want you to write about something difficult that happened to you each day. It doesn't matter how big or small it was. How did you overcome it? Don't forget to write about the progress you have made so far!

MONDAY

TUESDAY

WEDNESDAY

THURSDAY

FRIDAY

SATURDAY

SUNDAY

don't forget...

NOTES

Talk It Out

Pain does not come neatly wrapped in a pretty package. It's challenging and chaotic. There may be times that you want to talk about it, but you don't know what to say or how to say it.

I used to be so afraid of sharing my feelings. I felt like I would be misunderstood or judged. I needed support but I did not know how to ask for it. For years, I was quiet. I didn't speak to anyone unless they spoke to me first. This drastically affected how I communicated with others. I remember one instance that I was talking with my husband. I tried to communicate how I felt but I didn't know how. I was emotionally and socially broken. My husband loved me enough to work with me and help me learn how to express myself again.

Processing trauma or pain means that you are trying to make sense of it. However, trauma doesn't make sense; it's full of painful, unspeakable emotions. The key to healing is to turn those unspeakable feelings into words. You can do this by talking to a therapist or trusted family or friends. One thing I found extremely helpful was journaling. Words have power and writing can be an essential tool in harnessing your voice.

However, the most effective tool on my journey has been prayer. God will heal and mend. It's what he does; it's who he is! You don't have to understand; you just have to trust him!

When God heals and restores, he brings you out better than you were before.

Reflection

Do you have a trusted source to talk about your issues? If not, how do you express yourself?

_____
_____
_____
_____
_____
_____
_____
_____
_____
_____
_____
_____
_____

Look to the LORD and his strength; seek his face always

1 Chronicles 16:11

QUOTE OF THE DAY

"*The most **important** thing in **communication** is to hear what isn't being said.*"

TODO I AM GRATEFUL FOR:

HEALING AFFIRMATION

I CREATE LOVING AND HEALTHY RELATIONSHIPS

WRITE YOUR OWN AFFIRMATION

NOTES

> **PEOPLE START TO HEAL THE MOMENT THEY FEEL HEARD.**

Choose to Forgive

Who do you need to forgive?

Write down how this person's actions have caused you pain. What steps can you take to move forward? Don't worry if you are not yet ready to forgive. You are making progress by taking the first step!

AFFIRMATIONS

How you speak to your inner child is extremely important. Positive affirmations help you to release negativity, fear, worry, and pain. When you constantly repeat these affirmations they begin to take charge of your thoughts, slowly changing your pattern of thinking and ultimately changing your life. Fill in the boxes below with affirmations that you would say to your younger self.

EXAMPLE:

THIS IS NOT YOUR FAULT

Do It For You

Healing is a journey that you have to sometimes take alone. No one will ever be as invested in your life as you will. You have to make a conscious effort to better yourself each day.

When I first started my journey, I wanted to show everyone that I had changed. I spent a lot of years hurting those around me. I pushed them away so they wouldn't see how broken I was. The more God worked on me and changed my heart, I wanted the world to know. The problem was, my healing was based on the acceptance and approval of others. I became frustrated because they did not respond as I thought they should. Their rejection made me feel as if I had failed. My wound was gone but I still had a scar. I was still carrying the old mindset into a forced reality. I became so focused on showing others I was healed that I stopped healing.

Healing has to be for YOU! It can be a long journey but the result is worth it. Our wounds are often the opening into the best and most beautiful part of us. The more I worked on healing; I discovered the beauty that lied in my brokenness. Truth is, just because you have been broken doesn't mean you are forgotten. It's in those moments of brokenness that you discover your true power.

I realize now that I was made for more. My purpose was greater than my pain! I did it for me and God used it to work for me!

Reflection

How can you remain focused on your healing? What have you found out about yourself during this journey?

_____
_____
_____
_____
_____
_____
_____
_____
_____
_____
_____
_____
_____
_____
_____

And we know that all things work together for good to those who love God, to those who are called according to his purpose"

Romans 8:28

QUOTE OF THE DAY

""The wound is the place where the light enters you."

TODAY I AM GRATEFUL FOR:

HEALING AFFIRMATION

I LET GO OF MY PERCEIVED PAIN

WRITE YOUR OWN AFFIRMATION

NOTES

> **BE YOU.
> DO YOU.
> FOR YOU.**

Weekly Goals

Last week you worked on forgiveness. This week I want you to focus on accountability. Write down one way each day that you are going to hold yourself accountable. Don't forget to write about how you are feeling this week!

MONDAY

TUESDAY

WEDNESDAY

THURSDAY

FRIDAY

SATURDAY

SUNDAY

don't forget...

Healing Over Everything

There will be times on this journey that you have to intentionally choose healing. You have to put forth the daily effort to remain whole. There will always be someone who remembers who you were. However, you have to KNOW who you are now!

I can remember going to the local fair with my husband. We ran into some individuals who were familiar with my family. We walked over and they introduced me to the group they were with as a "Harris." The group just looked at me and gasped because apparently, that name had a negative condescendence. At that moment, I had two choices. I could let it affect me or keep moving forward. I chose the latter. I smiled and greeted them with love. I am not going to say it didn't initially hurt, because it did. It's hard to heal when you are constantly reminded of your wound. However, I knew then what I know now; I am loved! God loves me and you more than we will ever know. The great thing about him is, he doesn't hold it against us. He knows what we are going to do before we do it. He is aware of our situation and he only asks that we surrender to him.

You will always have naysayers, doubters, and haters. Healing is a choice! You have to choose HEALING OVER EVERYTHING! It won't always be easy and it will take work to change your bad habits. However, keep making the choice and I promise you will begin to see a shift in your mindset and your life.

Remember, your purpose is hidden within your wounds!

Reflection

What things have you been putting over your healing? How can you change this?

_____
_____
_____
_____
_____
_____
_____
_____
_____
_____
_____
_____
_____
_____
_____

I lift my eyes to the hills – where does my help come from? My help comes from the Lord, the maker of heaven and earth.

Psalm 121 1-2

QUOTE OF THE DAY

"If you want to heal your heart's wounds, start healing your thoughts."

TODAY I AM GRATEFUL FOR:

HEALING AFFIRMATION

==I GIVE MYSELF PERMISSION TO DO WHAT IS RIGHT FOR ME==

WRITE YOUR OWN AFFIRMATION

NOTES

> **THE EMOTION THAT CAN BREAK YOUR HEART IS SOMETIMES THE VERY ONE THAT HEALS IT.**

Weekly Goals

You made it through another week of healing. This journey of healing is a choice! Write down how you intentionally chose to heal each day. Don't forget to write about the progress that you have made so far.

MONDAY

TUESDAY

WEDNESDAY

THURSDAY

FRIDAY

SATURDAY

SUNDAY

don't forget...

Break The Cycle

Do you find yourself repeating cycles when it comes to your healing? The trauma from your childhood may be hiding in your daily actions. This affects your mindset and causes you to make unhealthy choices.

Trust was always a huge issue for me. I had a hard time opening up to others in fear they would eventually hurt me. I wasn't comfortable sharing my heart with someone who would try to use it against me someday. I would go into isolation and completely shut down if anyone got too close. I didn't realize it then, but this was hidden childhood trauma. When I was bullied in school, I would hide in the bathroom. I would sit in there for much of my lunch break, just to escape.

Somehow, that habit of isolation found its way into my adult life. I didn't deal with the trauma and I definitely wasn't interested in healing from it. I guess I was hoping it would just go away. *However, a wound left untreated can affect your entire body.* It started to interfere with my relationships and my mindset. I had to break the cycle! I refused to continue living a life of dysfunction. I learned a new way to live rather than repeating what I had already lived through.

You have already learned how to acknowledge the pain and let go of the past. Now you must break the cycle. You can't change the past, it happened. You have to heal yourself to make sure that the pain stops with you! We talk about breaking generational curses but let's take it one step further.

Let's work to make sure we don't create any new ones for generations to come!

Reflection

What cycles do you need to break in your life?

_____
_____
_____
_____
_____
_____
_____
_____
_____
_____
_____
_____
_____
_____

Whoever conceals his transgressions will not prosper, but he who confesses and forsakes them will obtain mercy.

Proverbs 28:13

QUOTE OF THE DAY

"Although the world is full of suffering, it is full also of the overcoming it."

TODAY I AM GRATEFUL FOR:

HEALING AFFIRMATION

I AM FREE FROM THE WOUNDS OF MY PAST

WRITE YOUR OWN AFFIRMATION

NOTES

"WE REPEAT WHAT WE DON'T REPAIR."

Weekly Goals

You're almost there! You have taken several steps toward healing your inner child. This week, write down one thing you have learned on your journey. How did you incorporate this into you daily life? Don't forget to write about something good that happened to you this week!

MONDAY

TUESDAY

WEDNESDAY

THURSDAY

FRIDAY

SATURDAY

SUNDAY

don't forget...

Reclaim Your Power

Healing allows you to reclaim your power. It allows you to put the broken pieces back together and become stronger than you were before. Healing changes your narrative from victim to survivor.

A victim is defined as a person who is harmed as a result of an event or action. For many years, I was a victim of my pain. I let it dictate how I interacted with others and how I lived my life. It stripped me of my happiness, joy, and power. I didn't know how to manage without the bubble of trauma that surrounded me. I had to take back my power. *There was too much purpose in my story to be silenced by my pain.*

I have said this in almost every devotional and I'm saying it again; HEALING IS A PROCESS! I did not wake up one day completely healed and whole. I had to intentionally choose each day to work on myself! I didn't always get it right, some days I failed. There were times I didn't feel that I could ever pull myself out of this broken place. It was in those low moments that I was reminded I wasn't alone. I didn't have to do it on my own. God was and has been there every step of the way. His strength was made perfect in my weakness. His grace and power brought my broken heart to rest. Not only was God beside me but he was also ahead of me. He cleared a path for me, all I had to do was keep moving forward.

When everyone else gave up on me, he restored me! He can do the same for you but you have to put in the work!

Reflection

What have you given your power to? What steps can you take to get it back?

_____
_____
_____
_____
_____
_____
_____
_____
_____
_____
_____
_____
_____
_____

He heals the brokenhearted and binds up their wounds.

Psalm 147:3

QUOTE OF THE DAY

"Your Journey Belongs to YOU."

TODAY I AM GRATEFUL FOR:

HEALING AFFIRMATION

I AM POWERFUL

WRITE YOUR OWN AFFIRMATION

NOTES

> "YOU RECLAIM YOUR POWER BY LOVING WHAT YOU WERE ONCE TAUGHT TO HATE."

HEALING GOALS

There is no time limit to healing. However, you can set mini goals to work towards it. List goals you want to improve on during your healing journey.

GOAL	TIME FRAME NEEDED	ACTIONS TAKEN TO ACHIEVE GOAL
I will engage in one self-care activity	*1 week*	*Write down a list of self-care activities I would like to do*

Rewrite Your Story

My prayer is that this devotional has given you the tools to continue your journey. As I have stated, healing is a process! You are well on your way to being fully healed and whole.

How do you want your story to end? Rewrite it below!

Dear Young Me,

Right now, you are fearless. You are not concerned with how others perceive you. Keep it that way! Don't worry about pleasing anyone except God! Never lose your smile, no matter what. Even though society may say differently, know that you are beautiful! I must warn you, there will be times that others will make fun of you. They will talk about you for your size and tease you because you have a gap in your teeth. They will make fun of the way you dress and speak. They will talk about you behind your back. Don't let this get to you and whatever you do don't stay silent!! Don't allow the opinions of others to define who you are. You are beautifully and wonderfully made. Truthfully, some days the weight of being constantly ridiculed will get to you. However, don't stay in that moment. You will cry, you will feel pain but DO NOT let it overcome you.

You must realize that your pain is designed to press you into your purpose. There will be times that you feel misunderstood but that's OK. There will also be times that you feel alone and that's OK too! Know that God is always with you. He will never leave you or forsake you. You will go through many trials in your lifetime. You will be hurt and lose ones that are dear to you. Do not let this get you down! Life's trials will test you, and shape you, but don't let them change who you are! There is no need to go and search for love. God loves you more than you know! God is love. It is what he is. So remember that no matter how alone you may feel, God is there and he loves you just the way you are.

My most important advice for you is to never dim your light to let others shine. If they do not accept you for who and what you are, let them go! You are smart! You are talented! Your opinions matter! Your voice matters! You playing small doesn't serve the world. There's nothing enlightening about shrinking so others won't feel insecure around you. As you let your own light shine, you indirectly give others permission to do the same. Be you, always!

Love,

Joy

Use this space to continue to journal your progress!

www.ingramcontent.com/pod-product-compliance
Lightning Source LLC
Chambersburg PA
CBHW052342100426
42736CB00047B/3420